© CapChord, 2024. All rights reserved.

No part of this publication may be reproduced, distributed, or transmitted in any form or by any means, including photocopying, recording, or other electronic or mechanical methods, without the prior written permission of the publisher, except as permitted under the Copyright Act or under terms agreed upon in writing.

It should be noted that certain images contained within this book are subject to separate licencing agreements and may not be reproduced without adhering to their respective terms and conditions.

It is important to acknowledge that the content presented herein does not necessarily reflect the viewpoints of the publisher.

About The Author

Pam Carter is a member of the Deo Gloria Community Church. In her spare time, she enjoys painting, travelling, writing poetry, gardening, and spending time with her family.

She lives with her husband, Philip, and has three children and six grandchildren. She considers her church community an extension of her family.

Acknowledgements

I would like to acknowledge the work of my grandson Declan in compiling and publishing this edition.

I would also like to thank Alanna Carter for her work on the first edition and my church family for their encouragement and support.

TABLE OF CONTENTS

Foreword	5
Be Refreshed	6
No Change	8
Almighty God	10
Worship	12
A Mother	14
Follow Him	16
Come And See	18
Children	19
Depend on Jesus	20
Jesus is Watching	21
Love	22
New Year	24
Open My Eyes	26
Palm Sunday	27
Our Busy Lives	28
Perseverance	30
Suffering	32
Some Reflections	33
Spiritual Flatness	34
Stand Up For Jesus	36
Today	38
The Christian Task	39
The Colours of Creation	40
The Lord Jesus	42
The Power Of The Tounge	44
No Room for Jesus	46
This Day	48
Christmas Time	49
Easter	50
Father's Day	51
Special Days	52

This book is dedicated to my dearest granddaughter, Lenae, who is beginning her walk with the Lord.

Foreword

I have called my third book of spiritual poems 'Be Refreshed,' because often on life's journey we need to stop, take stock of our lives, get our priorities right, and refresh our thoughts. It seems that our lives are so full of things to be done that we often become overwhelmed with the pressures of our day-to-day activities. Being occupied and busy is not necessarily a bad thing, as long as we have time for the important things in life.

Ecclesiastes 3:1 tells us, "There is a time for everything, and a season for every activity under the heavens...". In the eyes of a Christian, the most important thing in life is our relationship with Jesus Christ, our Lord and Savior. Jesus is with us throughout our busy days, watching over us and waiting for us to go to Him. Never be so busy that you don't have time to find a quiet place each day to talk to our Heavenly Father in prayer.

The time spent with our Lord is a time of refreshment, where the pressures of life melt away for a while as we renew our faith and strength. Psalm 46:1 tells us, "God is our refuge and strength..." Be refreshed in Him.

BE REFRESHED

2 Corinthians 3:18 - And we all, who with unveiled faces contemplate the Lord's glory, are being transformed into his image with ever-increasing glory, which comes from the Lord, who is the Spirit.

No matter just how strong our faith,
Or how earnest our prayer may be,
We need to reflect on Jesus,
So our Lord's glory we may see.

Go find a place of peace and rest,
To concentrate on God's way,
Remembering the many blessings
That Jesus sends us every day.

Be safe in our Lord's protection,
As we shelter under His wing,
For strength cling to Christ's strong right hand,
And joyful praises to Him sing.

We should never be too busy,
To talk to God and read His word,
So find each day a special time,
And let His love around you gird.

There are many kinds of people
Who can be helpful in our walk,
Meet in fellowship with others,
Who share our faith; listen and talk.

For in our wide church family,
There is someone to spur you on,
To encourage and be with you,
A friend we can rely upon.

At times when we get out of line,
A rebuker is what we need,
To gently guide us when we err,
Who we respect and truly heed.

We all need an intercessor,
A person who will pray for you,
And when we see someone in need,
We should intercede for them too.

A partner is someone special,
With whom we relax and share life,
Or with family or dear friend,
Who shares in happy times and strife.

Our pastor is there to listen,
When spiritual advice we need,
But most of all go to our God,
Who dwells with us all day indeed,

Yes, pause in serene reflection,
Meet with Jesus quietly each day,
Repent and read God's Holy Word,
And let God's Spirit show the way.

Do all these things and you will find,
You'll feel so refreshed and at peace,
Ready to face whate'er life brings,
As blessings from God never cease.

No Change

Isaiah 64:8 – Yet you, LORD, are our Father. We are the clay, you are the potter; we are all the work of your hand.

Embrace the changes that take place
Whether at home, church, work or play,
For changes bring variety,
That can lighten up our day.

Some changes are for the better,
While others aren't helpful at all,
But some things never change in life,
Being constant overall.

Like the sunrise in the morning,
And the sunset that comes at night,
The seasons; rain, sunshine and snow,
The darkness that follows light.

And promises that God gives us,
The truths found in His holy book,
The agony upon the cross,
That for our sins Jesus took.

His resurrection from the dead,
His promise of life forever,
To believers these things don't change,
His love it changes never.

Jesus is our glorified Lord,
And ruler of all creation,
He changes not and reaches out,
To each and every nation.

We know that God is the potter,
And we know that we are the clay,
This fact never changes at all,
As He moulds us day by day.

We are indebted to our God,
He was there at our very birth,
So let us glorify and praise,
Our God while here on earth.

The changes God has planned for us,
He will in time to us reveal,
Meanwhile embrace the life He gives,
And in prayer before Him kneel.

ALMIGHTY GOD

Job 11:7 – Can you fathom the mysteries of God? Can you probe the limits of the Almighty?

Almighty God who's there to save,
And helps me climb the highest wave,
Who cleanses my soul from within,
By His forgiveness of my sin.

Who knows the thoughts inside my heart,
And shows me how to do my part,
By leading me from place to place,
To tell His people of His grace.

Who loves me with a love so strong,
Who's there to teach me right from wrong,
Who's there for me both day and night,
Who keeps me always in His sight.

Who stands beside me when I'm down,
And wipes away my worried frown;
Who grants to me an inner peace,
Who shows me blessings that don't cease.

Who's been with me before my birth,
Who's in control of all the earth,
Who in splendour made creation,
And did design every nation.

Almighty God who's three in one,
Father, Spirit, Jesus His Son,
Humbly I bow on bended knee
With thanks for all you do for me.

WORSHIP

1 Chronicles 16:29 – Worship the LORD in the splendor of his holiness.

Bow down and worship before your God,
And with wonder His praises do sing,
Ascribing all honour and glory
To His majesty the sovereign king.

So worthy of worship is your God,
And through worship your faith will grow,
Until your whole life is full of praise
For almighty God who loves you so.

Say, here I am to worship you Lord,
And feel His love and His grace so true,
Connect with God with all of your heart,
As the Holy Spirit flows through you.

Worship your God in spirit and truth,
Listen quietly to God's inner voice,
Invest for a life in the Kingdom,
As with conviction you make your choice.

Kneel down before your infinite God,
Worship in His wondrous creation,
Whether with others or all alone,
Worship with love and adoration.

The outcome of worship will bring you,
A strength and a peace so sublime,
That you'll reach for the deepness of worship,
As the ladder of God's word you'll climb.

So worship the God of all nations,
And rejoice as you call on His name
Declare your faith in humble reverence,
As you worship the Lord who does reign.

A Mother

Proverbs 1:8 & 9 - ...do not forsake your mother's teaching. They are a garland to grace your head...

A mother forgets childbirth pains,
When she feels her newborn's touch,
As gently in her arms she holds
Her baby she loves so much.

A mother's hands they are outstretched,
As she's there for that first walk,
And listens very carefully,
When her child begins to talk.

She's ready to be firm but fair,
When tantrums her toddler takes;
She's there to help when her child falls,
With a kiss she better makes.

A mother takes her child to school,
And is there to reassure,
When all is strange, new and unknown,
And the child feels so unsure.

A mother is there with answers,
To help when her child's in strife,
She's there to teach of everything,
That will help her child through life.

Mums have God given qualities,
As the Lord God did intend,
Protective and kind and caring,
When her child hurts she does mend.

Some mums need help to raise a child,
Through her prayers God hears her needs,
So thank you God that we have mums,
Tales of God she tells and reads.

Always there to keep her child safe,
Teaching the right way to go,
To nurse and comfort when they're sick
And watch o'er them as they grow.

The Lord does love all the children,
This is God's gift to mothers,
Though many children she may have,
Loves daughters and their brothers.

Mothers aren't there for one season,
Or just when a child is small;
A mother's love is forever,
'Til she hears God's trumpet call.

These words remind me of God's love,
For He's with us from our birth,
And always watches over us,
As we live upon His earth.

His hands they are ever ready,
To uplift us when we fall,
And He's always there to listen,
When in prayer to Him we call.

The Lord is there with discipline,
When we wander from the track,
And when we ask for forgiveness,
He always welcomes us back.

When we face problems or trouble,
And fret, stress and worry too,
God is there, always beside us,
Helping us to see things through.

When we do not have an answer,
Then go down on knees and pray,
Listen to the Holy Spirit
Closely to what he may say.

God's love is not for a season,
His love lasts for evermore,
All through life how long that may be,
Til He calls us to His door.

Follow Him

1 John 2:2 - He is the atoning sacrifice for our sins, and not only for ours but also for the sins of the whole world.

Jesus will never leave us, He's in the world today,
And though we may not see Him, He's there to guide our way.
He suffered and He died on that cross so long ago,
He died to free us from our sins because He loved us so.
Jesus was resurrected to show the world for sure,
That there is life eternal, if we knock on our Lords door.
He bids us all to enter, and to seek freedom from sin,
For no one will be turned away if we just follow Him.
God in His mighty wisdom to earth His son He sent,
To save the souls of sinners if to Him they would repent.

Come And See

John 14:23 - Jesus replied, "Anyone who loves me will obey my teaching. My Father will love them, and we will come to them and make our home with them."

God promises all of His children
To come to Him, - when it's time, - to see,
The wonderful place in His Heaven,
He's prepared for you and me.

Yes, God has made a heavenly home,
And bids the faithful Christian to come,
To reside with Him in perfect peace,
When their work on earth is done.

Children

Mark 10:16 – And he took the children in his arms, placed his hands on them and blessed them.

Each child is like a shining jewel
Twinkling brightly in the sun,
Lighting up a world in darkness,
Bringing joy to everyone.

With their innocence and wonder,
They gathered around Christ's knee,
And as the scriptures do tell us,
He said, 'Let them come to me.'

The children of God's Kingdom,
Are so precious in His sight,
It is up to us to lead them
Down the pathway that is right.

So tell them stories of Jesus,
Of His life when here on earth,
How what He said is all truth still,
Though told years before their birth.

Children are thirsty for knowledge,
And so eager to be taught,
So teach them by your example,
Christlike truths just as we ought.

For children they are so trusting,
And never too young to know,
The wonder of our Heavenly Lord,
And how much he loves them so.

DEPEND ON JESUS

Acts 17:28 – For in him we live and move and have our being.

By His grace we live and move
And have our very being,
He supplies the air we breathe
And gives our lives true meaning.

We look to Him for our needs,
Our food, shelter, health and life,
And know he's there to comfort
When we go through trials and strife.

God's there when we face problems,
As we travel down life's road,
He sustains us when we fall,
And helps us to bear the load.

We can depend on His word,
And within each and every page,
We find a verse of comfort,
No matter the time or age.

Jesus shows many blessings
Even though we don't deserve.
Depend on Him who gives us life,
For His goodness our Lord serve.

Serve Him with a contrite heart,
Not because we think we ought,
But with a sense of wonder,
Share with others what he taught.

JESUS IS WATCHING

Psalm 121:3 - He who watches over you will not slumber...

Jesus is patiently watching
For the sinner to come to Him,
He lets it be known he is there
And is ready to say, 'come in'.

No matter the time they are calling,
Or how old the person may be,
He's standing there with open arms,
Saying, 'child just come here to me'.

He is always there to welcome,
Anyone who comes to repent,
Asking for sin to be lifted;
His forgiveness is Heaven sent.

The angels rejoice in Heaven,
When Jesus saves another soul,
New Christians will thank Lord Jesus,
For being born again and whole.

LOVE

1 Corinthians 13:13 – And now these three remain: faith, hope and love. But the greatest of these is love.

There are so many kinds of love,
But all have a common story,
Of kindness, patience, selflessness
And guiding others to God's glory.

Many attributes we may have,
As gifts from our dear Lord above,
Like faith and hope and empathy,
But the greatest of all these is love.

There's the love for fellow Christians,
Who are as sister and brother,
For as our Lord commanded us,
We should care for and love each other.

Some in today's society,
Have run amok and are so wild,
They may seem to us unlovely,
But remember all are our Lord's child.

We may see them as unworthy,
Loving them may be hard to do,
But take the time and shun them not,
Sharing with them what God's done for you.

Cultivate the love you do have,
For your spouse with a love so dear,
Have respect for your differences,
And draw closer as year follows year.

Your children need a special love,
One of guidance and protection,
As from a baby they do grow,
You shower them with great affection.

Display a love to all fellow men,
Whether they are stranger or friend,
Be gently kind in all you do,
As a Godly message you do send.

The greatest love that is given,
Comes from our Lord Jesus on high,
So with our mind and strength and heart,
We should love as to Him we draw nigh.

NEW YEAR

Jeremiah 29:11 - "For I know the plans I have for you," declares the LORD

A new year is just beginning,
The old one has passed away,
How should we greet this brand new year
As it breaks on a new day?

Let's greet it with expectation
Of exciting times ahead,
And walk along the narrow way,
Taking heed what the Lord said.

Be with the Lord God this new year,
Whatever may you befall,
Just be ready to do God's will,
When your heart does hear Him call.

Be positive and raise your head,
Sing praises to God's glory,
Encourage others as you go,
Tell them of God's great story.

Be a bright light in the darkness,
Shine with a positive light,
Bringing smiles and joys to others,
Keep Jesus always in sight.

But most of all be so thankful,
Every day of this new year,
For all the Lord has done for you,
And for being always near.

We know not what the new year brings,
The future isn't ours to know,
But with Christ as our cornerstone,
Trust and praise for Him will flow.

Open My Eyes

Psalm 119:18 – Open my eyes that I may see wonderful things in your law.

Open my eyes that I may see,
The wonder of life you gave to me,
The beauty of nature that doth surround,
Your awesome creation seen all around.

Open my ears that I may hear,
The great wonders of truth that draws me near,
Words from you when to this world you came,
And now in heaven forever you reign.

Open my mouth that I may speak
Of you my God, so others may seek;
Let all my words be told true and right,
So people will know the truth of your light.

Open my hands that I may feel,
Your very presence as to you I kneel,
Make me aware of your touch so sure,
As I walk towards your wide open door.

Open my heart that I may know,
My personal Saviour whom I love so,
You died on the cross to set me free,
From all of my sins that so burdened me.

Open my mind and God intrude,
Please give my being the right attitude
So that I may be worthy of you,
In all that I say and all that I do.

Palm Sunday

Matthew 21:9 - "Hosanna to the Son of David!" "Blessed is he who comes in the name of the Lord!" "Hosanna in the highest heaven!"

As Jesus drew near to Jerusalem,
He did send two disciples ahead,
To fetch from a village a donkey,
Then to Jesus the donkey was led.

The disciples laid cloaks on the donkey,
And Jesus climbed on the donkey's back,
Setting off for the nearby city,
Following along a well worn track.

The onlookers jostled to see Him,
Casting cloaks and Palm leaves on the road,
As the donkey did travel onward,
Carrying Jesus, its precious load.

As He came near the Mount of Olives,
The whole crowd raised voices to say,
"Peace in Heaven and glory on high,
Blessed is the King passing our way."

Jesus approached the city and wept,
For the sin was abundant and rife,
Christ knew that soon He'd die for men's sin,
Offering believers eternal life.

Our Busy Lives

Deuteronomy 6:12 - ...be careful that you do not forget the LORD...

I wake up in the morning
And already my day is planned,
For there's so very much to do
As I take all the jobs in hand.

I have a hurried breakfast,
Then pull the vacuum from its nook,
Push the cleaner round the house,
Then from the cupboard duster took.

When the house has been cleaned up,
I drive off to the local shop,
To buy more food and pay some bills,
No time to chat or look or stop.

Now it's on to the next thing,
For there's phone calls I have to make,
Then gather up ingredients
For the cake I promised to bake.

It is time to do the garden
And take grandchildren to the zoo,
For my daughter is so busy
And mum has little she must do!!

Returning home exhausted,
There is dinner now to be cooked,
But just before I get started
There's an appointment to be booked.

A hurried meal then wash up,
And it's off to my evening class;
I don't feel much like studying,
But if I don't then I won't pass.

At last I'm home for a while,
And I fall thankfully into bed,
One more busy day is over
And I can rest my weary head.

But as I lay in the dark,
The pastor's words come back to me,
"Don't be so bound to the urgent
That the important you don't see.

What could be more important,
Than my dear Saviour's saving grace?
And though He's been with me all day,
I've not left time my Lord to face.

So when I wake tomorrow,
Before I start my hectic day,
I'll read His word and be refreshed,
As I come to my Lord and pray.

So Father please forgive me,
For my dire neglect of you,
Let all my days from this day on,
Be lived for you my whole day through.

And though I may be busy,
As my routine demands of me,
I'll keep the important in sight,
So your light I may always see.

PERSEVERANCE

Hebrews 10:36 – You need to persevere so that when you have done the will of God, you will receive what he has promised.

Run with hope and perseverance,
The road that is mapped out for you,
Always fix your eyes on Jesus,
In all you say and all you do.

Whatever you set out to do,
If your project is God's will,
Then Jesus will work beside you,
And will be helping you until

The job has been accomplished,
Be it at home or church or play,
So don't give up but persevere,
As you do work from day to day.

Things may seem a long time coming,
Your patience may be growing thin,
But all in God's time you will find
The outcome you will surely win.

God knows those who do persevere,
And suffer hardship for His sake,
So in your troubles trust the Lord,
As His will you do undertake.

In your doctrine and in your life,
May your faith continue to grow,
Persevere with trust and kindness,
With love for others as you go.

So look forward to your future,
Where your hope it is true and sure,
You'll receive what God has promised,
A life with Him for evermore.

SUFFERING

Romans 8:18 – I consider that our present sufferings are not worth comparing with the glory that will be revealed in us.

God didn't promise us all through this life,
That we would be free from all suffering and strife,
Or that at times we would face deep despair,
But He did promise that He'd always be there.

God didn't promise from pain we'd be free,
But Jesus did tell us to, 'Come unto me.'
So go to the Lord with problems and grief,
Sharing with the Saviour will bring such relief.

Suffering can bring us back to the Lord's way,
If we've wandered from Him and been led astray,
Draw close to God, bring before Him your woes,
For how you suffer our Lord truly knows.

Problems in sickness, or grieving or doubt,
Whatever the anguish God will sort it out,
For suffering of all kinds takes many a road;
Talking to Jesus will lighten the load.

Faith can be strengthened when put to the test,
Look unto the Lord to bring you peace and rest,
He'll walk with you when you stumble or fall,
Whatever the suffering on you may befall.

We face sorrow but mercy does abound,
For on the horizon in our Lord is found,
A place for us where there's freedom from pain,
Where the Almighty God forever will reign.

Some Reflections

Be near me Lord and let me see
Your bright shining light guiding me,
Stay with me Lord and forever be
My personal Saviour who set me free.

***

Jesus came into my life when I was very small,
I first heard of His wondrous grace when at Sunday School,
I heard how He was always there to help me when I fall,
Though years have passed and I'm now old He's still my all in all.

***

Walk with God along His road,
Allow Him to share your heavy load,
He'll guide you as you go on your way,
Until you are in His arms to stay.

***

Show me the way to Calvary,
Where Jesus Christ he died for me,
Show me the way to serve Him best,
Before I lay me down to rest.

***

Guard my mouth so when I speak,
The words that from me flow,
Bring comfort and show our Lord's love,
Wherever I may go.

Spiritual Flatness

Galatians 1:6 – I am astonished that you are so quickly deserting the one who called you to live in the grace of Christ...

Sometimes a spiritual flatness
Just seems to overtake me,
I fight these inner shackles
As I strive to be set free.

Feel like ranting and raving,
I wonder what I should do,
My faith is being tested,
There's only flatness in view.

I wander round in circles,
I cry out to God at night,
Please fill my heart Lord Jesus
And make everything alright.

Where is the Holy Spirit?
In my soul I cannot feel,
Is this the work of Satan,
Robbing me of fire and zeal?

Oh no! That cannot happen,
I fall on my knees to ask
Jesus to take the darkness
So in His light I may bask.

It's then a miracle happens,
And calmness envelopes me,
As Christ touches me lightly
And reopens my eyes to see

That never did He leave me,
Just sat by my side to wait,
'Til he saw me on the road
Heading for His open gate.

With arms of love wide open,
I run into His warm embrace,
And thank Him with all my heart
For His great mercy and grace.

Stand Up For Jesus

1 Corinthians 15:58 – Therefore, my dear brothers and sisters, stand firm. Let nothing move you.

'Stand up, Stand up for Jesus,'
A hymn well known to all,
Remember Christ your Saviour,
Whatever may befall.

'Stand up, Stand up for Jesus,'
Whenever others mock,
Let your Lord God sustain you
For you are of His flock.

'Stand up, Stand up for Jesus,'
And let your faith shine through,
Tell others of your Saviour
And what he's done for you.

'Stand up, Stand up for Jesus,'
When non Christians are around,
Be not moved by ridicule,
Show your belief is sound.

'Stand up Stand up for Jesus,'
And open up your heart,
Ask what the Lord wants from you.
How can you do your part?

'Stand up, Stand up for Jesus,'
And say a silent prayer,
For people who are hurting,
That they may know God's care.

'Stand up, Stand up for Jesus,'
And to His word be true,
Display fruits of the Spirit
In all you say and do.

'Stand up, Stand up for Jesus,'
Be worthy of His name,
Tell how to save poor sinners
Our Lord and Saviour came.

TODAY

Matthew 6:11 – Give us today our daily bread.

Another day has started, it's time for me to rise,
To throw back the covers and to open up my eyes.
We may have plans and organised just how the day will go,
But God is watching o'er us and only He does know.
We may just have a happy day or maybe one of care,
But however the day unfolds we know the Lord is there;
And when the day is ended and it is time for bed,
We thank the Lord for this day as we lay our weary head.

The Christian Task

Acts 20:24 – However, I consider my life worth nothing to me; my only aim is to finish the race and complete the task the Lord Jesus has given me...

Each one of us was chosen by God,
To do for His glory a task,
If you're not sure what God wants from you,
Get down on your knees and ask.

Just open your heart to Lord Jesus,
And listen to what he does say,
For the Holy Spirit within you,
Will guide you in the right way.

Sometimes you may not have realised;
So think back on your life on earth,
And look at work you did long ago
For God planned it at your birth.

For some it will be a lifetime task,
For others one allotted thing,
But for all of the Lord God's children
He asks other souls to bring

To the waiting arms of Christ Jesus,
And to tell them right from the start,
Of the wonderful love abundant,
And peace He'll bring to their heart.

THE COLOURS OF CREATION

Colossians 1:16 - For in him all things were created...

The beauty of our Lord God is shining all around,
In every bird and flower His glory can be found.
Every petal and each leaf gleams freshly bold and bright,
The sun and moon above pierce darkness with God's light.

Endless colours seen with a variety of hue,
Beasts and birds and plants are God's precious gift to you.
The sweet smells of new mown hay and the rain after the dry,
The roses on the bush and the pretty butterfly.

Herds of grazing cattle, woolly sheep safe in the fold,
Horses in the paddock are a great sight to behold.
Autumn leaves so lovely, in colours of golden brown,
And orange, red and yellow caught on a breeze drift down.

The redness of the soil and the whiteness of the sands,
Meet blue and aqua sea that surrounds God given lands.
The white tipped surf that tumbles on every distant shore,
Sometimes lapping gently, sometimes with a roar.

The colours in the rocks, and the mountains rising high,
The bats and bees and ants, and the blueness of the sky,
The water in the streams, the drop of a waterfall,
The vast expanse of ocean; the Lord God made them all.

The splendour of a sunset of orange, pink and red,
Heralds the end of day when creation rests its head.
The wonder of a sunrise and golden sunny ray,
Awakening God's world as night fades to a new day.

The Lord Jesus

James 1:17 – Every good and perfect gift is from above...

Who holds you in a warm embrace?
Who pours on you abundant grace?
Who loves you with abiding love?
Who cares for you from heaven above?
The Lord Jesus

Who shows you mercy without end?
Who forever is our best friend?
Who changes not from day to day?
Who watches as we go our way?
The Lord Jesus

Who walks with us on life's long road?
Who when we hurt will share our load?
Who knows the thoughts within our heart?
Who forgives when our sins impart?
The Lord Jesus

Who listens to us when we pray?
Who promises with us to stay?
Who lifts us up on eagle's wings?
Who to our life peace and joy brings?
The Lord Jesus

Who's Spirit does within us dwell?
Who asks that others we should tell?
Who caused us to be born again?
Who over the whole world does reign?
The Lord Jesus

Who shows compassion when we grieve?
Who does our leaden heart relieve?
Who lifts us up when we are down?
Who wipes away our every frown?
The Lord Jesus

Who came to earth and is God's Son?
Who over death a victory won?
Who from our sins did set us free?
Who in eternity we'll see?
The Lord Jesus

The Power Of The Tounge

Philippians 2:11 - ...and every tongue acknowledge that Jesus Christ is Lord...

Our tongue is like a flame of fire,
Which can be used against our brothers,
But wisely used and you will find,
It can encourage and warm others.

What do your words convey to God
When you kneel down before Him to pray?
Do all your words come, through the heart
Showing love and praise in what you say?

Use your tongue to uplift others,
When they are low their self worth renew,
Tell them how much God does love them,
And understands what they're going through.

Don't compromise on your standards,
When some non-believers are around,
But with your words and with actions,
Display how your faith in God is sound.

The tongue's a powerful organ,
Has abilities to change a life,
It can bring peace, joy or sorrow,
Happiness and elation or strife.

It's our responsibility,
For as a Christian it is our role,
To know the 'Fruit of the Spirit,'
And over our tongue use self control.

Keep your eyes always on Jesus,
Read and listen to what He does say,
Be tuned into God for guidance,
And you could lead one to God today,

Be ever alert for Satan,
For your words he will try to distort,
Think well before you use your tongue,
Hold onto integrity of thought.

It's not just having the knowledge,
That the teacher is remembered for,
But how knowledge was delivered,
Is what will make a man thirst for more.

Use words to each other kindly,
And in gossip never take a part,
With your words don't hurt Lord Jesus,
For it's the tongue that reveals the heart.

Be gracious towards each other,
Be helpful in thought, word and deed,
Use your tongue to tell of Jesus,
And thank God for His grace indeed.

So think of words before you speak,
Consider how well you use your tongue,
Let all you say, and all you do,
Bring all honour to God's risen Son.

No Room for Jesus

Luke 2:7 - She wrapped him in cloths and placed him in a manger, because there was no guest room available for them.

God looked down on a broken world,
And sent His son to show the way,
His name was the Lord Jesus Christ,
Born on the very first Christmas Day,

He wasn't born in a palace,
With riches, robes and jewels galore,
Our King was born in a stable,
And lay in a manger on some straw.

There was no room for our dear Lord,
Every Inn in the town was full,
The only place He could be born
Was with some animals in their stall.

And so on down through the ages,
Christians are oft' saddened to find,
That there's still no room for Jesus,
For many he's never brought to mind.

In many schools the Lord's shut out.
They say theres no room for Him there
Why teach of Biblical Guidance,
When for Jesus they really don't care!

And then within the government,
They say, it's not politically correct
To follow Godly principles,
For other beliefs it may affect.

No room for Christ in the workplace,
No time to take hold of His hand,
Only produce and money matters,
In places of toil throughout the land.

Arrangements keep folk so busy,
With Christmas gifts, baubles and fare,
And as the family gathers round,
Do they know why they are there?

Do they say, 'No room for Jesus',
In their home on this Christmas day,
Or will they open their door wide
And invite Jesus Christ in to stay?

In your house is there always room?
As you celebrate is God a part?
Do you thank Jesus for Christmas,
Really mean it deep down in your heart

Christmas is just the beginning,
Of our Saviour's wondrous story,
Of how God sent His only Son,
To show us the way to glory.

Yes, there should be room for Jesus,
In every Christian home that's true,
Not only at the time of Christmas,
But every day the whole year through.

This Day

Malachi 4:2 - ...the sun of righteousness will rise with healing in its rays.

This day is surely your day whatever your age,
Today in the Book of Life is another page.
So how will you use it? What will you do?
Will you make this day worthwhile and to God be true?
When you wake in the morning what will you say?
Will you say good morning Lord, thank you for today?
Or are you so busy that from your bed you leap,
Pulling on clothes and rubbing eyes full of sleep?
Today is a gift that the Lord does you bestow,
He will stay with you today wherever you may go.
So take a deep breath, Take time to look around,
At every blessing that God your life does surround.
Go about you business with lightness of feet,
Greet all with a smile whoever you chance to meet.
Whatever joys or trials this day may have in store,
Know God's in control, today and for evermore.

CHRISTMAS TIME

Isaiah 9:6 – *For to us a child is born, to us a son is given...*

Christmas time it is here again,
With excitement the children cry,
A time to decorate the tree,
Also to hang the tinsel high.

A time to write some Christmas cards,
And shop for presents at the store,
To put up lights around the house,
And hang a wreath upon the door.

A time to eat a Christmas feast,
Of turkey, pudding, cream and ham,
Then pack up for a holiday,
Joining the endless traffic jam.

Amidst of all this merriment,
Does the true meaning pass us by,
Do we pause; taking time to wonder,
What this time means to you and I.

For there wouldn't be a Christmas,
If God's son had never been born,
In a stable of a busy inn,
On the very first Christmas morn.

The dear baby's name was Jesus,
A precious gift God sent to earth,
For to teach and love and save us,
So let's remember our Lord's birth.

Let us all bow down and worship,
Ask the Lord Jesus to come in,
Open our lives and homes this Christmas,
And celebrate this time with Him.

EASTER

Matthew 28:6 - He is not here; he has risen, just as he said. Come and see the place where he lay.

E is for EASTER when over death our Lord won.
A is the AGONY suffered by Jesus, God's son,
S is for SACRIFICE when Christ died for our SIN,
T is the THIRD day when the TOMB was empty within.
E is ETERNAL life if you answer Gods call,
R is our RISEN Lord who reigns over all.

So remember at Easter God's great gift to you
And rejoice with thankful hearts in all that you do.

Father's Day

Proverbs 13:1 – A wise son heeds his father's instruction...

Fathers, they are special people,
Sent to us from the Lord above,
To protect and teach their children,
With kind discipline and love.

Fathers can do so many things,
Like giving piggy backs when small,
Or help to mend a broken toy,
And bring comfort when we fall.

They can tell such lovely stories,
When sitting snugly on their knee,
They tell us all about Jesus,
Of His love for you and me.

As we grow up the world changes,
And childish things we leave behind,
But lessons learned from fathers,
So often are brought to mind.

Our Heavenly Father tells us,
Always honour fathers on earth,
For He sent them to watch o'er us,
From the moment of our birth.

So on this day that's set aside,
Remember fathers young and old,
And ask our Lord to touch their hearts,
And in His arms tightly hold.

Special Days

EASTER
Time to reflect on our Lord's death,
As He was crucified so cruel,
Then rejoice for on the third day
He rose again the world to rule.

CHRISTMAS
A joyous season here again,
Lift up your hearts and sing,
Of our Lord's birth in Bethlehem,
As with love our gifts we'll bring.

NEW YEAR
A new year it has just begun,
Now time to start anew,
And ask forgiveness for past sins,
And to our God be true.

SPECIAL DAYS
Honour and respect your parents,
As God commanded you,
Be loving, kind and helpful,
In all you say and do.

Printed in Dunstable, United Kingdom